HOW TO SELL ON ETSY FOR BEGINNERS 2023

THE ULTIMATE GUIDE TO BEING A PROFITABLE SELLER ON ETSY

By Ella Nelson

CONTENTS

ABOUT THE AUTHOR

Meet Ella Nelson, a seasoned entrepreneur, creative maven, and Etsy aficionado. With her deep passion for handmade crafts and her extensive experience in the online marketplace, Ella has become a trusted authority on selling successfully on Etsy. Driven by her entrepreneurial spirit and a desire to share her knowledge with others, Ella devoted herself to mastering the intricacies of the Etsy marketplace. She delved into every aspect of running a successful shop, from perfecting product photography to mastering SEO optimization. Through trial and error, she honed her strategies, discovering the keys to attracting customers, increasing sales, and building a brand that resonates.

As an author, Ella's writing style is approachable, engaging, and infused with her infectious enthusiasm. She has a knack for breaking down complex concepts into simple, actionable steps that readers can readily implement. Her genuine passion for helping others succeed shines through as she shares practical advice, insider tips, and inspirational stories of Etsy entrepreneurs who have turned their dreams into reality.

With a keen eye for trends and a finger on the pulse of the Etsy community, Ella stays up-to-date with the evolving landscape of the online marketplace. She understands the challenges and opportunities that arise in this ever-changing digital world and provides timely insights to help readers navigate with confidence.

Beyond her expertise in selling on Etsy, Ella embodies the spirit of community and collaboration that Etsy champions. She actively engages with fellow sellers, participates in forums, and organizes workshops to foster connections and support others on their entrepreneurial journeys. Her dedication to empowering individuals to turn their passions into profitable businesses is the driving force behind her writing.

Whether you're a budding artist looking to monetize your creations or an established seller seeking to optimize your shop, Ella Nelson's book on selling on Etsy is your go-to resource. Prepare to be inspired, equipped with practical strategies, and guided by an author who understands the magic and potential of the Etsy platform. Through Ella's guidance, you'll gain the tools to unlock your own success story on Etsy's vibrant stage.

INTRODUCTION

In a world dominated by mass production and impersonal retail experiences, Etsy stands as a beacon of creativity, individuality, and community. It is a vibrant online marketplace where artisans, crafters, and vintage collectors from around the globe come together to share their passions, showcase their skills, and connect with like-minded individuals. Welcome to "How to sell on Etsy for beginners."

Within the pages of this book, we embark on a journey through the fascinating world of Etsy—a place where handmade crafts, unique creations, and vintage treasures find their rightful homes. Whether you're a creative soul eager to turn your hobby into a thriving business or a curious shopper seeking one-of-a-kind treasures, this guide is your ultimate companion.

Etsy is not just an ordinary e-commerce platform; it's a thriving ecosystem built on the pillars of creativity, craftsmanship, and community. We'll delve into the essence of Etsy, exploring its rich history, core values, and the vibrant community that fuels its success. You'll gain a deep understanding of how Etsy has revolutionized the way we connect with makers and the stories behind their creations.

But what makes Etsy truly special is the diverse array of products you can find within its virtual walls. From handcrafted jewelry that tells a personal story to vintage clothing that carries the whispers of bygone eras, every item on Etsy has a unique tale to tell. We'll explore the various categories and niches within the marketplace, giving you a glimpse into the vast world of possibilities that await you.

Whether you're a seller or a buyer, this guide equips you with the essential knowledge and strategies to navigate Etsy with confidence. We'll walk you through the process of setting up your shop, curating your inventory, optimizing your listings, and effectively promoting your brand. You'll learn invaluable tips and tricks from experienced sellers who have honed their skills and found success on Etsy's bustling platform.

For buyers, we'll uncover the secrets to finding hidden gems amidst the sea of options. We'll guide you in refining your searches, decoding product descriptions, and making informed purchasing decisions that align with your personal style and values.

Through "How to sell on etsy for beginners," you'll not only unlock the potential to build a thriving online business or discover extraordinary handmade and vintage treasures—you'll also become part of a passionate community that celebrates craftsmanship, supports small businesses, and embraces the beauty of the handmade.

So, whether you're a seasoned Etsy enthusiast or just embarking on your journey into the world of handmade wonders, prepare to be inspired, empowered, and enchanted. Welcome to a world where creativity knows no bounds and where dreams find their wings—welcome to Etsy!

WHAT IS ETSY?

Etsy is an online marketplace that focuses on the buying and selling of handmade, vintage, and unique items. It was founded in 2005 and has since become a popular platform for artisans, crafters, and small businesses to showcase and sell their products to a global audience.

On Etsy, you can find a wide range of items across various categories, including handmade crafts, artwork, jewelry, clothing, home decor, vintage items, and more. What sets Etsy apart is its emphasis on creativity, craftsmanship, and the personal stories behind each item. Many sellers on Etsy create one-of-a-kind or custom-made products, making it a go-to destination for people seeking unique and personalized goods.

Etsy provides an accessible platform for sellers to set up their own online storefronts, manage their inventory, and connect with potential buyers. Buyers, on the other hand, can explore a vast selection of distinctive products, connect with sellers, and support independent businesses.

The Etsy platform offers features such as search filters, reviews, secure payment options, and a community-driven environment that encourages engagement and interaction among buyers and sellers. It has gained a reputation for fostering a sense of community, supporting small businesses, and promoting sustainable and ethical shopping practices.

Buyers can browse through millions of listings on Etsy, discovering one-of-a-kind products that are not typically found in traditional retail stores. The platform allows users to search by category, location, price range, and other filters to find exactly what they're looking for. Etsy also promotes a sense of community by encouraging buyers to engage with sellers, leave reviews, and support independent businesses.

In its early days, Etsy started with a small community of sellers who primarily offered handmade crafts and vintage items. The founders aimed to create a platform that celebrated the beauty of handmade goods and connected artisans directly with buyers who appreciated their unique creations.

Etsy's growth gained momentum as word spread about the platform's commitment to supporting independent artists and offering a wide range of one-of-a-kind products. The company received its first major funding in 2006, allowing for further development and expansion.

Over the years, Etsy continued to evolve and adapt to the changing needs of its community. The platform introduced new features and tools to enhance the seller and buyer experience, including improved search capabilities, seller analytics, and a robust review system.

In 2015, Etsy became a publicly traded company, marking a significant milestone in its history. As the platform grew, it faced challenges in maintaining a balance between supporting small businesses and meeting the demands of a larger marketplace. Etsy implemented policies to ensure the authenticity of handmade items and to support environmentally conscious practices.

Today, Etsy has become a global e-commerce powerhouse, connecting millions of buyers and sellers from around the world. It remains a popular destination for those seeking unique, handmade, and vintage products, fostering a sense of community and supporting independent artisans and entrepreneurs.

Throughout its history, Etsy has stayed true to its founding principles of celebrating craftsmanship, promoting sustainability, and fostering a marketplace that values creativity and individuality. The platform continues to evolve and innovate, empowering sellers and providing a vibrant marketplace for buyers who appreciate the beauty and authenticity of handmade goods.

Overall, Etsy provides a marketplace where creativity thrives, and individuals can discover and purchase special items that reflect their unique style and values.

WHY SELL ON ETSY?

Selling on Etsy offers several benefits for artisans, crafters, and independent sellers. Etsy attracts a specific audience of buyers who are actively looking for unique, handmade, and vintage items. By selling on Etsy, you can reach a niche market that appreciates and seeks out the type of products you offer.

Etsy is a well-established and trusted online marketplace. It has been around since 2005 and has built a solid reputation among buyers. Selling on a platform with a strong brand presence can give your products added credibility and trustworthiness.

Setting up a shop on Etsy is relatively straightforward. The platform provides user-friendly tools and templates to help you create and customize your shop quickly. You don't need advanced technical skills or extensive web development knowledge to get started. Starting an Etsy shop has low entry costs compared to building your own e-commerce website or opening a physical store. Etsy charges nominal fees for listing products and takes a percentage commission when you make a sale. This makes it a cost-effective option for sellers, especially those starting out or operating on a smaller scale.

Etsy offers various built-in marketing and promotional tools to help you increase visibility for your products. You can optimize your listings with relevant keywords, take advantage of personalized recommendations, participate in seasonal campaigns, and utilize social media integration to reach a broader audience. Etsy has a thriving community of sellers who actively engage with each other, share knowledge, and offer support. You can join forums, teams, and groups to connect with like-minded individuals, gain insights, and receive guidance on various aspects of running an online business.

Etsy provides integrated payment processing, allowing you to accept multiple payment methods, including credit cards, PayPal, and Etsy gift cards. The platform also offers shipping tools and discounted rates with major shipping carriers, simplifying the shipping process for sellers. Etsy provides sellers with access to analytics and insights about their shop's performance. You can track views, favorites, and sales data, which can help you make informed decisions about pricing, inventory management, and marketing strategies.

In conclusion, Etsy has a global presence, allowing sellers to expand their customer base beyond their local market. You can potentially reach buyers from different countries and increase your sales opportunities. Etsy is constantly evolving and introducing new features and tools to enhance the seller experience. They regularly listen to feedback from sellers and make improvements to the platform. This ongoing development ensures that sellers have access to up-to-date resources and opportunities. Remember that success on Etsy still depends on factors such as the quality and uniqueness of your products, competitive pricing, effective marketing, and providing excellent customer service.

WHO CAN SELL ON ETSY?

Etsy allows individuals and businesses who create or curate handmade, vintage, or craft supplies to sell on its platform. Here's a breakdown of who can sell on Etsy:

Artisans and Crafters: If you create handmade items, such as jewelry, clothing, home decor, artwork, pottery, or any other unique crafted products, you can sell them on Etsy. The platform encourages sellers to offer items that are made by hand or involve significant handwork and craftsmanship.

Vintage Sellers: If you have vintage items that are at least 20 years old (as of the current year), you can sell them on Etsy. Vintage items can include clothing, accessories, home decor, collectibles, and more. These items should be accurately described and classified as vintage, not newly manufactured.

Craft Supplies: Etsy also allows sellers to offer craft supplies that are used for creating handmade items. These supplies can include materials like fabric, beads, yarn, paper, tools, and other components commonly used in crafting.

Collaborative Shops: Etsy allows multiple individuals to collaborate and sell together under a single shop. This option is useful for groups or teams of artists, crafters, or makers who want to pool their resources and create a collective shop.

It's important to note that sellers on Etsy are expected to comply with the platform's policies and guidelines. This includes accurately representing their products, providing excellent customer service, and following any specific regulations or laws related to their products or business operations.

Before starting to sell on Etsy, it's recommended to review their seller guidelines and policies to ensure that your products and business practices align with their requirements.

WHAT CAN YOU SELL ON ETSY?

On Etsy, you can sell a wide range of unique and creative products within the categories of handmade, vintage, and craft supplies. Here's a broad overview of the types of items you can sell on Etsy:

Etsy is known for its focus on handmade products created by artisans and crafters. You can sell a variety of handmade goods such as jewelry, clothing, accessories, home decor items, artwork, crafts, personalized items, and more. The possibilities are vast, limited only by your creativity and skills.

If you have vintage treasures that are at least 20 years old, you can sell them on Etsy. Vintage items can include clothing, accessories, jewelry, home decor, collectibles, vintage books, vinyl records, and more.

Vintage enthusiasts often search for unique finds, making Etsy an ideal platform for connecting with interested buyers.

If you offer materials and tools used for crafting, you can sell craft supplies on Etsy. This can include fabrics, beads, buttons, yarn, paper goods, sewing patterns, paint, brushes, knitting needles, and any other supplies that crafters may need to create their own handmade items.

Etsy also allows the sale of digital products, such as printable art, digital designs, patterns, templates, invitations, and more. These products can be downloaded by buyers upon purchase, providing a convenient and instant option for customers seeking digital goods.

Etsy is a popular platform for selling personalized and customized products. This can include personalized jewelry, custom-made clothing, monogrammed accessories, engraved items, custom illustrations, and other items tailored to the buyer's specifications.

Lastly, It's important to note that while these categories cover a broad range of items, there may be certain restrictions or guidelines specific to each category. Before listing your products on Etsy, make sure to review their policies and guidelines to ensure compliance and to understand any specific requirements for the type of items you plan to sell.

Additionally, it's a good idea to research existing sellers on Etsy within your niche or product category to gain insights into what types of products are popular and in-demand.

HOW MUCH CAN YOU MAKE SELLING ON ETSY?

The amount of money you can make selling on Etsy can vary greatly depending on various factors, including the quality and uniqueness of your products, pricing strategy, marketing efforts, customer demand, competition, and your overall business approach. Some sellers on Etsy achieve significant success and generate substantial income, while others may experience more modest earnings.

It's important to note that selling on Etsy, like any business venture, requires effort, dedication, and the ability to adapt and improve over time. Offering high-quality, well-crafted, and unique products can attract more buyers and potentially command higher prices, increasing your earning potential.

Setting prices that are competitive within your niche and market while considering factors such as material costs, labor, and profit margin is crucial. Carefully research similar products on Etsy to get an idea of the price range and adjust your pricing strategy accordingly.

Promoting your Etsy shop and products through effective marketing efforts can help increase visibility, attract more customers, and ultimately boost sales. Utilize social media platforms, engage with your target audience, collaborate with influencers or bloggers, and optimize your Etsy shop's SEO to improve discoverability.

High-quality product photos and detailed, compelling descriptions can significantly impact your sales. Invest time and effort into creating appealing visuals and accurately describing your products to capture the interest and trust of potential buyers.

Providing excellent customer service and building a positive reputation on Etsy can lead to repeat customers and positive reviews. Positive feedback and testimonials can enhance your shop's credibility and attract more buyers.

Staying informed about market demand and trends within your niche can help you identify popular products and capitalize on emerging opportunities. Regularly research and assess what customers are looking for to adjust your product offerings accordingly.

It's important to approach selling on Etsy with realistic expectations and understand that success and income levels can vary widely. Some sellers may generate a significant full-time income, while others may use Etsy as a supplementary source of income or a hobby-based business. Consistency, continuous improvement, and adapting to the market can contribute to your long-term success on Etsy.

SECTION 1
SETTING THE GROUNDWORK FOR SUCCESS ON ETSY.

CREATING AN ETSY ACCOUNT

Step 1: Visit The Etsy Website

Open your preferred web browser and go to the Etsy website www.etsy.com. On the Etsy homepage, locate the "Sign in" link usually located at the top right corner of the page and click on it.

Step 2: The Sign-up Process

On the sign-in page, you have two options to create your Etsy account: Sign in with Google or Facebook: If you have a Google or Facebook account, you can click on the respective buttons to sign in to Etsy using those accounts. This will link your existing Google or Facebook account to Etsy.

Step 3: Register for a new account

If you prefer to create a new Etsy account, click on the "Register" button located below the sign-in form. If you clicked on "Register," you'll be directed to the account registration page. Here, you will need to provide the following information:

Email address: Enter a valid email address that you have access to. This will be used for communication and account verification purposes.

Create password: Choose a strong and secure password for your Etsy account. Make sure to use a combination of letters, numbers, and symbols to enhance security.

Username: Create a unique username that will represent your shop and profile URL on Etsy. Choose a name that is memorable and reflects your brand or personal identity. After entering the required information, click on the "Register" button to proceed.

Step 4: Verification Process

Etsy will send a verification email to the email address you provided during registration. Go to your email inbox, find the email from Etsy, and open it. In the email, you will find a verification link. Click on the link to confirm your email address and activate your Etsy account. If the link doesn't work, you can copy and paste the provided URL into your browser's address bar.

Step 5: Language and Currency Confirmation

After verifying your email, you will be directed back to the Etsy website. At this point, you may be asked to choose your preferred language and currency for your Etsy account. Select your preferences and click "Save and continue."

Step 6: Addition of Profile Picture

Complete your Etsy profile by adding a profile picture. Click on the blank profile picture icon in the top right corner of the Etsy page, then choose

"Profile photo" from the drop-down menu. Upload a photo from your computer or choose one from your existing social media accounts.

Additionally, you can provide additional information about yourself and your shop by clicking on the "Profile" link in the same drop-down menu. Add details such as your bio, location, and any other relevant information that you'd like to share with potential buyers.

Congratulations! You have successfully created your Etsy account. You can now start exploring the various features and tools available to sellers on Etsy, set up your shop, and begin listing items for sale.

CHOOSING A SHOP NAME

Choosing a shop name on Etsy is an important step in creating your brand identity and attracting potential customers. Choose a shop name that reflects the essence of your business and the products you offer. It should align with your brand's style, values, and target market. Think about the overall image you want to convey to potential customers.

Select a shop name that is easy to remember and stands out from the crowd. A catchy and unique name can help you make a lasting impression and make it easier for customers to find and remember your shop. Your shop name should align with your brand identity, whether it's whimsical, elegant, vintage-inspired, or modern. Consider incorporating descriptive or evocative words that give potential customers an idea of what you offer. For example, if you sell handmade jewelry, including words like "jewelry," "handcrafted," or "artisan" in your shop name can help convey your niche.

Before finalizing your shop name, check its availability on Etsy. Make sure no other shop is using the same or a very similar name to avoid confusion or potential trademark issues. You can search for existing shop names on Etsy to ensure uniqueness. A shorter shop name is often easier to remember and type, making it more convenient for customers to find you. Avoid lengthy or complicated names that may be harder to remember or fit into promotional materials.

Including relevant keywords related to your products or niche in your shop name can help with search engine optimization (SEO) and improve your shop's visibility in Etsy's search results. However, be careful not to overstuff your shop name with keywords, as it should still sound natural and appealing.

If you plan to expand your product offerings in the future, consider choosing a shop name that is broad enough to accommodate potential growth. This allows you to diversify your product line without needing to change your shop name later. Once you have a few shop name options in mind, share them with friends, family, or trusted individuals to get feedback. They can provide insights and opinions that may help you make a final decision.

Remember, your shop name is an essential part of your brand identity, so take your time to choose a name that resonates with you and your target audience. Once you've settled on a name, you can proceed with creating your Etsy shop and start showcasing your unique products.

SETTING YOUR SHOP'S LOCATION AND CURRENCY

Setting your Etsy shop's location and currency accurately is crucial for providing a clear and transparent shopping experience for your customers. Here is a detailed step-by-step guide on how to set your Etsy shop's location and currency:

Step 1:Logging into your Etsy Account

Sign in to your Etsy account on the Etsy website www.etsy.com. Once logged in, click on the "Shop Manager" link located at the top right corner of the Etsy homepage. This will take you to your shop management dashboard.

Step 2: Locating the settings tab

In the Shop Manager, you will find a left-hand side menu. Locate and click on the "Settings" tab. Under the "Settings" menu, click on the "Info & Appearance" option. This will open the page where you can manage various shop settings, including location and currency.

Step 3: Changing Your Shop Location

On the "Info & Appearance" page, scroll down until you reach the "Shop Location" section. Here, you will see the current location information for your shop. If you need to update your shop's location, click on the "Change" button next to the existing location details. A pop-up window will appear, allowing you to enter your shop's new location. You can enter your specific address or simply provide the city or region where your shop is based. As you type, suggestions will appear, and you can choose the most appropriate option from the provided list. Once you have entered the new location information, click "Save" to confirm the changes. Your shop's location will now be updated.

Step 4: Changing Your Shop Currency

Scroll down further on the same page to the "Currency" section. Here, you can set the currency in which you want to display your prices and conduct transactions in your shop. Click on the drop-down menu under "Currency" and choose the currency that is most appropriate for your business. Select the currency you prefer to use for pricing your items and completing transactions with buyers. After selecting the desired currency, click "Save" to save your changes. Your shop's currency will now be updated.

However, It's important to note that changing your shop's currency will not convert your existing prices automatically. You will need to manually update your item prices to reflect the new currency if necessary.

By setting your Etsy shop's location and currency accurately, you ensure that your shop's information is displayed correctly to potential buyers. This helps them find your shop, understand the location from where your products are shipped, and view prices in their preferred currency. It also facilitates smooth and transparent transactions, contributing to a positive shopping experience for your customers.

ADDING YOUR PRODUCTS

Etsy is a popular online marketplace that allows artisans, crafters, and independent creators to sell their unique products to a global audience. Adding your products on Etsy is a straightforward process that involves creating a listing, optimizing it for visibility, and managing your inventory. This comprehensive guide will walk you through each step to ensure a successful product listing on Etsy.

1. Setting Up Your Etsy Shop:

Before adding products, you need to set up your Etsy shop.

a. Sign up: Visit Etsy's website (www.etsy.com) and click on the "Sell on Etsy" button. Create an account or sign in if you already have one.

b. Shop Preferences: Set your shop preferences, including your shop name, language, and currency. Consider choosing a name that reflects your brand or products.

c. Shop Policies: Define your shop policies regarding shipping, returns, and payment methods. Clear and concise policies build trust with customers.

d. Shop Banner and About Section: Customize your shop's appearance by adding a banner and writing an engaging "About" section to tell your story and showcase your products.

2. Creating a Product Listing:

Once your shop is set up, it's time to create a product listing.

a. Product Details: Click on the "Add a listing" button and provide accurate and detailed information about your product. Include the title, category, description, price, quantity, and variations (e.g., size, color).

b. Compelling Description: Craft a compelling and informative description that highlights the unique features, materials used, and potential uses of your product. Use keywords relevant to your product to improve search visibility.

c. High-Quality Photos: Include high-resolution, well-lit, and visually appealing photos of your product. Capture multiple angles and showcase any intricate details. Etsy allows up to ten photos per listing.

d. Pricing and Inventory: Set a competitive and profitable price for your product. Consider factors like production costs, time invested, and market demand. Keep track of your inventory to avoid overselling.

e. Shipping and Delivery Options: Specify shipping details, including shipping costs, processing times, and available shipping destinations. You can offer various shipping methods like standard, expedited, or international shipping.

f. Tags and Attributes: Utilize relevant tags and attributes to help customers find your product. Choose descriptive keywords that accurately represent your product, its style, and potential uses.

g. SEO Optimization: Optimize your listing for search engine optimization (SEO) by using keywords in the title, description, and tags. This increases the likelihood of your products appearing in relevant search results.

h. Preview and Publish: Review your listing using the preview feature to ensure accuracy. Once you're satisfied, publish your listing to make it live on Etsy.

3. Managing Your Listings and Shop:

After adding your products, it's essential to manage your listings and shop effectively.

a. Regular Updates: Periodically review and update your listings to reflect any changes in inventory, pricing, or product descriptions. This helps keep your shop fresh and up-to-date.

b. Marketing and Promotion: Promote your products through various channels, including social media, email marketing, and collaborations with influencers. Utilize Etsy's built-in marketing tools and consider paid advertising options for greater visibility.

c. Customer Communication: Respond promptly to customer inquiries, order messages, and feedback. Excellent customer service builds trust and encourages repeat purchases.

d. Analyze Shop Stats: Use Etsy's shop analytics to gain insights into your shop's performance. Monitor sales, traffic sources, and customer behavior to make informed business decisions.

e. Enhance Your Shop: Continuously improve your shop's appearance and branding. Consider adding additional shop sections, updating your banner, or creating a cohesive visual identity.

Adding your products on Etsy requires careful attention to detail and strategic optimization. By following the steps outlined in this comprehensive guide, you can create compelling product listings, enhance visibility, and manage your Etsy shop successfully. Remember to regularly update your listings, stay engaged with customers, and explore marketing opportunities to grow your business on Etsy.

SETTING UP SHIPPING OPTIONS

Setting up shipping options on Etsy is an essential part of managing your shop. Etsy provides a flexible and customizable shipping system that allows you to set shipping costs, specify processing times, and define shipping destinations. Here's a step-by-step guide on how to set up shipping options on Etsy:

1. **Sign in to your Etsy account:** Go to www.etsy.com and log in to your seller account. Then you access Shop Manager by clicking on your profile picture at the top right corner of the page, and select "Shop Manager" from the drop-down menu.

2. **Open Shipping Settings:** In the Shop Manager, locate the "Settings" tab on the left-hand side menu. Click on it to expand the options and then select "Shipping settings."

3. **Create a Shipping Profile:** Etsy allows you to create multiple shipping profiles, which can be useful if you offer different shipping methods for various products. If you haven't created a shipping profile yet, you'll be prompted to set one up. Click on "Add a shipping profile" to get started.

4. **Shipping Options:** Once you've created a shipping profile, you can define the shipping options within it. Here's how:

a. Shipping Destinations: Choose the countries or regions where you're willing to ship your products. You can select specific countries or opt for worldwide shipping.

b. Shipping Methods: Etsy provides several pre-set shipping methods, such as standard, expedited, or priority mail. You can choose from these options or create your custom shipping methods. Consider offering multiple options to cater to different customer preferences.

c. Shipping Costs: Specify the shipping costs associated with each shipping method. You can set flat rates, calculated rates based on package weight or dimensions, or offer free shipping. Ensure that your pricing covers packaging materials, handling fees, and any additional costs.

d. Processing Time: Define the processing time, i.e., the time it takes for you to prepare the order for shipping. It's important to set realistic processing times to manage customer expectations.

e. Package Details: Provide accurate information about the package size and weight. This helps in calculating accurate shipping costs, especially for carriers that charge based on package dimensions.

f. Additional Services: Etsy allows you to offer optional services like insurance, tracking numbers, or signature confirmation for an extra fee. Consider whether these services align with your shipping strategy and customer needs.

g. Save Changes: After setting up your shipping options, click on "S
to apply the changes to your shipping profile.

5. **Assign Shipping Profiles to Listings:** Once you have created shipping profiles, you need to assign them to your product listings. To do this: Go to the "Listings" tab in your Shop Manager, Edit the listing you want to assign a shipping profile to, Scroll down to the "Shipping" section of the listing editor, Choose the appropriate shipping profile from the drop-down menu, Save your changes.

6. **International Shipping:** If you're offering international shipping, it's important to be aware of customs requirements, import duties, and any restrictions specific to certain countries. Clearly communicate these details in your shop policies to avoid any confusion or issues.

7. **Review and Update:** Regularly review your shipping options to ensure they align with your business needs. Update your shipping profiles as necessary, especially when there are changes in carrier rates or your shipping strategy.

By following these steps, you can set up shipping options on Etsy that align with your business requirements and provide clarity to your customers regarding shipping costs, delivery times, and destinations. Remember to communicate any updates or changes in your shop policies to maintain transparency and customer satisfaction.

CUSTOMIZING YOUR STOREFRONT

Customizing your storefront on Etsy allows you to create a visually appealing and unique brand identity, making a positive first impression on potential customers. By customizing elements such as your shop banner, logo, sections, and policies, you can create a cohesive and memorable shopping experience.

First and foremost, Sign in to your Etsy account Visit www.etsy.com and log in to your seller account. Click on your profile picture at the top right corner of the page, and select "Shop Manager" from the drop-down menu.

Step 1: Customize Your Shop Appearance:

a. Shop Banner: In the Shop Manager, locate the "Settings" tab on the left-hand side menu. Click on it and select "Info & Appearance." Scroll down to the "Shop Banner" section and click on "Change Banner" to upload a custom banner image. Ensure that the banner represents your brand aesthetic, displays your shop name or logo prominently, and reflects the overall vibe of your products.

b. Logo: To add a logo, go to the "Info & Appearance" section in Shop Manager. Click on "Change Logo" and upload an image that represents your brand. This logo will appear alongside your shop name on various parts of your storefront, including your shop page and listings.

c. Shop Sections: Organize your products into sections to enhance navigation and improve the shopping experience. To create sections, go to the "Listings" tab in Shop Manager. Click on "Add a section" and give it a descriptive name. You can create multiple sections to categorize your products by type, theme, or any other relevant criteria. Drag and drop listings into the respective sections to organize them.

d. Featured Listings: Consider showcasing specific products as featured listings. To do this, go to the "Shop Manager" and select the "Listings" tab. Find the listing you want to feature and click on the three dots (...) next to it. From the dropdown menu, select "Add as featured listing." Featured listings will appear prominently on your shop page, attracting attention from potential customers.

e. Shop Policies: Ensure your shop policies are clear, concise, and easy to understand. Go to the "Settings" tab in Shop Manager, select "Info & Appearance," and scroll down to the "Shop Policies" section. Click on "Edit" to update your policies regarding shipping, returns, payment methods, and any other relevant details. Transparent and well-communicated policies build trust with customers.

f. Profile and About Section: Personalize your shop's profile and "About" section to provide customers with insights into your brand, inspiration, and values. Go to the "Settings" tab in Shop Manager, select "Info & Appearance," and scroll down to the "Shop Owner" section. Click on "Edit" to update your profile picture, location, and other details. Additionally, craft an engaging and informative "About" section that tells your story, showcases your expertise, and connects with your customers.

Step 2: Shop Announcement

Consider adding a shop announcement to highlight special offers, promotions, or important updates. To set up a shop announcement, go to the "Settings" tab in Shop Manager, select "Info & Appearance," and scroll down to the "Shop Announcement" section. Click on "Edit" to write a concise and attention-grabbing message. Update it periodically to keep your customers informed about any relevant news or events.

Step 3: Preview and Publish

Before finalizing your customizations, preview your shop to ensure that everything looks as desired. Click on the "Preview" button to see how your storefront appears to visitors. If you're satisfied with the changes, click on "Publish" to make your customizations live on Etsy.

Step 4: Regular Updates and Maintenance

As your business evolves, it's important to periodically review and update your storefront. Keep your banner, logo, sections, policies, and shop announcement fresh and relevant. Regularly evaluate your branding and make adjustments as needed to reflect your evolving brand identity and align with customer expectations.

By following these steps and customizing your storefront on Etsy, you can create a visually appealing and cohesive brand presence that attracts customers, builds trust, and encourages them to explore your products further. Remember to maintain consistency, regularly update your shop, and showcase your unique brand identity throughout your storefront.

GOING LIVE!

Going live on Etsy refers to officially launching your shop and making your products available for purchase to the public. Before going live, ensure that you have completed the necessary steps to set up your Etsy shop. This includes creating an Etsy seller account, defining your shop preferences, setting up shop policies, customizing your storefront, and adding your product listings. Refer to the relevant sections in this guide for detailed instructions on each step.

It's crucial to review and optimize your product listings to maximize their visibility and appeal. Double-check that all the information provided in your listings, such as product descriptions, prices, variations, and shipping details, is accurate and up to date.

Ensure that your product photos are of high quality, well-lit, and visually appealing. Showcase different angles, details, and variations if applicable. Optimize your listings for search engine visibility by incorporating relevant keywords in titles, descriptions, tags, and attributes. This helps potential buyers find your products when searching on Etsy.

Evaluate your pricing strategy and ensure that your prices are competitive and aligned with market standards. Keep track of your inventory to avoid overselling and manage customer expectations. Update your listings promptly if a product becomes unavailable.

To receive payments from customers, you need to set up your preferred payment methods on Etsy. Etsy provides options such as Etsy Payments (which includes various payment methods like credit/debit cards, PayPal, Apple Pay, etc.) or standalone PayPal. Choose the payment methods that work best for your business, set up the necessary accounts, and link them to your Etsy shop.

Set up your shipping options to provide accurate shipping costs, processing times, and available shipping destinations to your customers. Follow the steps outlined in the "Setting up Shipping Options on Etsy" section of this guide for detailed instructions on how to set up your shipping preferences.

Before going live, it's a good practice to conduct a test transaction to ensure that your payment and shipping processes are functioning correctly. Purchase one of your own products or ask a friend or family member to make a test purchase. This helps you identify any issues or gaps in the customer experience.

Review your shop settings one last time before going live. Verify that your shop name, logo, banner, sections, policies, and announcements are accurate and align with your branding and business goals. Make any necessary adjustments to ensure consistency and professionalism.

When you are satisfied with your shop setup, listings, payment methods, and shipping options, it's time to go live. To activate your shop and make it publicly accessible: In Shop Manager, go to the "Settings" tab, Click on "Options" from the left-hand side menu, Scroll down to the "Shop Status" section, Click on the "Open" button to activate your shop and make it live on Etsy.

Congratulations! Your shop is now live on Etsy, and customers can start exploring and purchasing your products. Also it's crucial to actively promote your shop to attract customers and generate sales. Utilize various marketing strategies such as social media, email marketing, collaborations with influencers, and Etsy's built-in marketing tools. Regularly analyze your shop's performance using Etsy's analytics and make adjustments to your marketing efforts as needed.

Remember to continuously update and improve your shop, add new products, respond promptly to customer inquiries, and provide exceptional customer service to enhance your shop's success on Etsy.

SECTION 2

OPTIMIZING YOUR ETSY SHOP FOR SEARCH

USING KEYWORDS AND TAGS

Keywords and tags play a crucial role in optimizing your listings on Etsy and improving their visibility in search results. When used effectively, keywords and tags can help potential buyers find your products more easily. In this explanation, I'll provide a detailed overview of how to use keywords and tags on Etsy.

Keywords are specific words or phrases that describe your product. They are the terms that potential buyers are likely to search for when looking for products similar to yours. Use keywords that accurately describe your product, including its attributes, materials, colors, and any unique features. Think about what words a buyer would use to search for your item.

Start by brainstorming a list of relevant keywords. You can also use tools like Google Trends, Etsy's own search bar, or keyword research tools like Marmalead or eRank to identify popular and relevant keywords for your product.

Consider using long-tail keywords, which are more specific phrases that target a niche audience. For example, instead of "handmade soap," you can use "organic lavender-scented handmade soap."

Etsy provides data on how often your listing appears in search results and how many views and sales it generates. Monitor this data and adjust your keywords accordingly to improve your listing's performance.

Tags are another important element of Etsy's search algorithm. They help categorize and organize your listings within Etsy's marketplace. Etsy allows you to use up to 13 tags per listing. Take advantage of this by using as many relevant tags as possible. Utilize all available tag slots to increase the visibility of your products. If your product has multiple variations, such as different colors or sizes, make sure to include tags for each variation. This ensures that your product appears in search results for all relevant options.

Use a mix of broad and specific tags. Broad tags may attract a larger audience, while specific tags can help you target a niche market. For example, if you're selling handmade jewelry, you can use broad tags like "necklace" or "bracelet," as well as specific tags like "boho jewelry" or "dainty gold necklace."

Stay up-to-date with current trends and seasons. If there are specific events, holidays, or trends that align with your product, include relevant tags to increase your chances of appearing in related searches. Explore Etsy's search bar or use tools like Marmalead or eRank to identify popular tags within your niche. Incorporate these tags into your listings to improve their visibility.

While it's important to use relevant keywords, avoid overloading your titles, tags, and descriptions with excessive keywords. This can negatively impact your search rankings and make your listings less appealing to buyers. Use consistent keywords across your titles, tags, and descriptions. This helps Etsy's algorithm understand the relevance of your listing and ensures your product appears in the most relevant search results.

Regularly review your shop's performance using Etsy's analytics tools. Pay attention to which keywords and tags are generating the most views and sales. Adapt your listings accordingly to maximize their effectiveness. As trends and search algorithms change, make sure to stay informed about any updates related to keywords and tags on Etsy. Join seller forums, follow Etsy's blog, or participate in relevant communities to stay up-to-date with the latest best practices.

Optimizing your keywords and tags on Etsy requires continuous refinement and adaptation. By using specific, relevant, and diverse keywords and tags, you can increase the visibility of your listings, reach a wider audience, and improve your chances of making more sales on the platform.

USING ATTRIBUTES

Attributes on Etsy refer to the specific characteristics or properties of a product that can be selected by buyers when they are making a purchase. Using attributes on Etsy is an effective way to provide additional details about your products, allowing potential buyers to easily filter and find exactly what they're looking for. Attributes are specific characteristics or options that define your products, such as size, color, material, style, and more. Utilizing attributes effectively can enhance the visibility of your listings and improve the overall shopping experience for potential customers.

Attributes are structured data fields that provide standardized information about your products. They help buyers refine their search results and make informed purchasing decisions. Each product category on Etsy has a set of specific attributes associated with it. For example, in the clothing category, attributes might include size, color, and material, while in the jewelry category, attributes might include metal type, gemstone, and length.

Start by identifying the attributes that are most relevant to your products. Consider the key characteristics that buyers might search for when looking for items like yours. It's essential to choose attributes that accurately describe your products and align with what customers expect.

Once you've identified the relevant attributes, fill in the attribute details for each product listing. Etsy provides a standardized format for entering this information. You'll typically find attribute fields within the listing creation or editing process. Depending on the category, you may have dropdown menus, checkboxes, or text fields to fill in the attribute details.

When filling in the attribute details, be accurate and descriptive. Provide as much relevant information as possible to help buyers make informed decisions. For example, if you're selling clothing, include details such as the fabric type, care instructions, and measurements. If you're selling artwork, provide details about the medium, dimensions, and framing options.

Ensure that you fill in all the available attributes relevant to your product. Leaving attribute fields blank may lead to your product not appearing in relevant search filters or missing out on potential buyers who specifically filter by those attributes. Utilize all the options provided by Etsy to provide as much information as possible.

If your product has variations, such as different sizes, colors, or styles, make use of the variations feature on Etsy. This allows you to create separate listings for each variation and specify the unique attributes for each one. Buyers can then choose the specific variation they want to purchase. Using variations helps buyers find exactly what they're looking for and enhances their shopping experience.

As your inventory changes or you introduce new products, make sure to review and update your attributes accordingly. Regularly check that the attribute details are accurate and reflective of the current state of your products. This ensures that your listings continue to provide accurate information and appear in relevant search filters.

Attributes can also contribute to the overall search engine optimization (SEO) of your listings. By including relevant keywords within your attribute details, you can potentially improve your product's visibility in search results. However, avoid keyword stuffing and maintain a natural and descriptive tone.

Using attributes effectively on Etsy enhances the shopping experience for buyers by providing detailed and specific information about your products. It allows them to filter their search results and find products that meet their preferences. By accurately and comprehensively filling in attribute details, you can improve the visibility and discoverability of your listings, potentially leading to more sales and satisfied customers.

KEEPING YOUR SHOP UP TO DATE

Keeping your Etsy shop up to date is essential for the success and growth of your online business. Regularly updating your shop helps you maintain a fresh and appealing storefront, attract customers, and stay competitive within the Etsy marketplace.

1. **Inventory Management:**

   - Regularly review and update product listings: Ensure that your product listings have accurate descriptions, pricing, and availability.
   - Remove sold-out or discontinued items: Keep your inventory up to date by promptly removing listings for products that are no longer available.

- Add new products: Continuously add new items to your shop to keep it interesting and attract returning customers.
- Consider seasonal or trending items: Stay aware of market trends and add products that align with popular demand or upcoming seasons.

2. **Pricing and Promotions:**

- Monitor market trends: Regularly review pricing strategies and adjust them to stay competitive in the market.
- Offer promotions and discounts: Attract customers by running sales, discounts, or bundle deals to encourage purchases.
- Review pricing competitiveness: Keep an eye on competitor pricing to ensure that your prices are reasonable and competitive.
- Test different pricing strategies: Experiment with different pricing strategies to find the optimal balance between profitability and customer appeal.

3. **Product Photography:**

- Ensure high-quality images: Use clear, well-lit, and professional product photos that accurately represent your items.
- Consistent branding: Maintain a consistent visual style and branding across all product images to create a cohesive and professional look.

- Update product images: If you make improvements or changes to your products, update the images to reflect their current appearance accurately.

- Lifestyle or styled photos: Consider incorporating lifestyle or styled photos to showcase your products in real-life settings or demonstrate their versatility.

4. Descriptions and Keywords:

- Optimize product descriptions: Write detailed and compelling descriptions that accurately highlight the features and benefits of your products.

- Incorporate relevant keywords: Research and use relevant keywords in your titles, descriptions, and tags to improve search visibility.

- Regularly review and update descriptions: Ensure that your product descriptions are up to date, accurate, and free from errors.

- Highlight updates or improvements: If you make any updates or improvements to your products, mention them in the descriptions to attract buyers.

5. Shipping and Policies:

- Review and update shipping options: Regularly evaluate and update your shipping options and rates based on carrier changes or your business needs.

- Communicate shipping and processing times: Clearly state your shipping and processing times in your listings to manage customer expectations.

- Keep policies up to date: Review and update your shop policies, including return and exchange policies, to reflect any changes or new information.

- Address customer concerns: Regularly review customer feedback and questions to address any recurring concerns or provide clarification in your policies.

6. **Customer Engagement:**

- Promptly respond to inquiries and messages: Engage with potential buyers and existing customers by promptly responding to messages and inquiries.

- Provide excellent customer service: Offer helpful and friendly customer service to ensure a positive buying experience.

- Engage through social media or newsletters: Connect with your customers through social media platforms or email newsletters to keep them updated about your shop and promotions.

- Collect and respond to feedback: Regularly collect and analyze customer feedback to understand their needs, address issues, and improve your products or services.

7. **Storefront Optimization:**

- Update shop banner and logo: Keep your shop's banner and logo up to date to reflect your brand identity and make a strong first impression.

- Organize shop sections: Arrange your shop sections in a logical and easy-to-navigate manner to help customers find what they're looking for.

- Add a shop announcement: Utilize the shop announcement feature to share important updates, promotions, or any other relevant information.

- Review and update shop policies and profile: Regularly review and update your shop policies, about section, and profile information to keep them accurate and informative.

8. Analytics and Data Analysis:

- Regularly review shop analytics: Utilize Etsy's analytics tools to track and analyze your shop's performance, including views, visits, and sales.

- Analyze customer behavior and preferences: Gain insights into your customers' preferences, including popular products, traffic sources, and conversion rates.

- Adjust strategies based on data insights: Use the data and analytics to make informed decisions about product selection, pricing, promotions, and marketing strategies.

- Utilize additional analytics tools: Consider using external analytics tools like Google Analytics to gain deeper insights into your shop's performance and customer behavior.

9. Stay Informed:

- Keep up with Etsy announcements: Stay updated with Etsy's news, policy changes, and new features by regularly checking Etsy's announcements or subscribing to seller newsletters.

- Participate in seller forums and communities: Engage with other Etsy sellers in forums or communities to learn from their experiences, share insights, and stay updated with industry trends.

- Follow industry trends: Stay informed about industry trends, new techniques, or emerging markets to adapt your shop's strategies accordingly.

- Continuous education: Invest time in learning and staying up to date with marketing, SEO, and e-commerce best practices to optimize your shop's performance.

Regularly keeping your Etsy shop up to date ensures that your listings are accurate, appealing, and competitive, ultimately attracting more customers and driving sales. By implementing these practices and staying proactive in managing your shop, you'll be on the path to maintaining a successful and thriving Etsy business.

PROVIDING GOOD CUSTOMER EXPERIENCE

Providing good customer experience on Etsy is crucial for building a strong reputation, increasing customer satisfaction, and fostering repeat business. Here are some key practices to ensure a positive customer experience:

Clear and Accurate Product Listings:

❖ Provide detailed and accurate descriptions of your products, including dimensions, materials, and any customization options.

❖ Use high-quality product images that showcase your items from various angles and accurately represent their appearance.

❖ Clearly state any policies or important information related to shipping, returns, or exchanges.

Prompt and Professional Communication:

❖ Respond to customer inquiries, messages, and reviews promptly and courteously.

❖ Be professional, helpful, and friendly in all your communications.

❖ Address any customer concerns or issues in a timely and efficient manner.

Fast and Reliable Shipping:

❖ Ship orders promptly within the specified processing times.

- ❖ Use reliable shipping methods and provide tracking information to customers whenever possible.
- ❖ Clearly communicate any delays or issues that may affect the shipping timeline.

Packaging and Presentation:

- ❖ Ensure that your products are well-packaged to protect them during transit and enhance the unboxing experience.
- ❖ Consider adding a personalized thank-you note or a small extra touch to surprise and delight your customers.
- ❖ Use branded packaging materials to reinforce your brand and leave a positive impression.

Quality Products and Craftsmanship:

- ❖ Strive to deliver high-quality products that meet or exceed customer expectations.
- ❖ Pay attention to detail and maintain consistency in the craftsmanship of your items.
- ❖ Use quality materials and conduct thorough quality control before shipping products.

Honesty and Transparency:

❖ Be transparent about your products, including any limitations, potential variations, or imperfections.

❖ Clearly state your shop policies, such as return or refund policies, to set proper expectations for customers.

❖ If there are any delays or issues with an order, promptly communicate with the customer and provide updates.

Post-Purchase Follow-up:

❖ Reach out to customers after their purchase to express gratitude and check their satisfaction.

❖ Encourage customers to leave reviews or provide feedback on their experience.

❖ Address any post-purchase concerns promptly and professionally.

Continuous Improvement:

❖ Regularly review customer feedback and use it to improve your products, services, and overall customer experience.

❖ Seek opportunities to innovate, introduce new designs or features, and stay ahead of customer expectations.

❖ Stay informed about industry trends and incorporate them into your products and customer service.

Going the Extra Mile:

❖ Surprise and delight customers by exceeding their expectations whenever possible.

❖ Offer personalized recommendations or assistance based on their preferences or previous purchases.

❖ Provide exceptional customer service even after the sale, ensuring a positive overall experience.

Remember, providing a good customer experience is not a one-time effort but an ongoing commitment. By consistently delivering excellent service, maintaining open communication, and continuously improving your products and processes, you'll establish a loyal customer base and foster a positive reputation on Etsy.

ENCOURAGING BUYERS TO LEAVE REVIEWS

Encouraging buyers to leave reviews on Etsy is essential for building social proof, gaining credibility, and attracting new customers. Positive reviews not only boost your shop's reputation but also improve your visibility in Etsy's search rankings.

1. Provide Exceptional Customer Service:

Offer outstanding customer service throughout the entire buying process. Respond promptly to inquiries and messages, addressing any concerns or questions. Go above and beyond to ensure customers have a positive experience with your shop.

2.   Send a Thank-You Note:

Include a personalized thank-you note with each order, expressing your appreciation for their purchase. Politely request that they leave a review if they are satisfied with their item and shopping experience.

3.   Encourage Communication:

Include a friendly message in your order confirmation or shipping notification, encouraging customers to reach out if they have any feedback or questions. Let them know that you value their opinion and would love to hear about their experience.

4.   Follow Up After Delivery:

Send a follow-up message after the estimated delivery date to ensure the item has arrived safely. Politely ask if they are happy with their purchase and kindly request a review if they are pleased.

5.   Offer Incentives:

Consider offering a small incentive for leaving a review, such as a discount on their next purchase or a coupon for future orders. Make sure to comply with Etsy's policies regarding incentives for reviews.

6.   Showcase Positive Reviews:

Display positive reviews prominently in your shop's announcements or product listings. Highlight the positive feedback you've received to showcase the quality of your products and customer service.

7. Make It Easy to Leave a Review:

Include a direct link to the "Leave a Review" section in your follow-up messages or thank-you notes. Make the review process as straightforward as possible to encourage participation.

8. Stay Courteous and Grateful:

Remember to remain respectful and appreciative when asking for reviews. Avoid pressuring customers or using overly pushy language.

9. Engage on Social Media:

Use your social media platforms to share positive reviews from satisfied customers. Mention that leaving reviews on Etsy helps small businesses like yours thrive.

10. Be Responsive to Reviews:

Respond promptly and graciously to any reviews you receive, whether positive or negative. Use negative feedback as an opportunity to address concerns and showcase your commitment to customer satisfaction.

Remember, the key to encouraging buyers to leave reviews is to provide exceptional products and service consistently. Positive reviews will naturally follow when customers have a great experience with your shop. Additionally, fostering open communication and expressing genuine gratitude for their feedback will further motivate customers to leave reviews and help your Etsy shop flourish

SECTION 3

MARKETING YOUR ETSY SHOP

Unlock the potential of your creative business with strategic Etsy shop marketing! Showcase your unique products to a wider audience by optimizing your product listings with relevant keywords and engaging descriptions. Leverage social media platforms to build a strong brand presence and connect with your target audience. Implement eye-catching visuals, share behind-the-scenes stories, and offer exclusive promotions to entice customers. Utilize Etsy's advertising options to boost visibility in search results and gain exposure to millions of shoppers. Engage with your customers, respond to inquiries promptly, and encourage positive reviews to build trust and loyalty. With a well-rounded marketing approach, watch your Etsy shop flourish as you attract more buyers and nurture a thriving online business.

USING ETSY'S MARKETING TOOLS

Etsy's marketing tools offer sellers powerful ways to increase their shop's visibility, reach a larger audience, and drive more sales. With these tools, sellers can promote their unique products effectively and maximize their Etsy shop's potential.

Empower your Etsy business with the advanced marketing tools provided by the platform. Etsy's marketing tools offer a comprehensive suite of features designed to boost your shop's exposure and attract more customers. Utilize Promoted Listings to place your products at the top of search results and target specific keywords to reach the right audience. With Etsy Ads, tap into Etsy's extensive network of shoppers through off-site ads, only paying when you make a sale from these promoted listings.

In addition to paid advertising, Etsy's marketing tools also enable sellers to leverage social media platforms. Easily share your products on Instagram, Facebook, and Pinterest directly from your shop, expanding your reach to new potential buyers and increasing brand visibility. Engage with your audience through engaging posts and stories to build a loyal following.

Etsy's marketing dashboard provides valuable insights into the performance of your ads, helping you refine your strategies for maximum effectiveness. Monitor the return on investment (ROI) of your marketing efforts and make data-driven decisions to optimize your ad spending.

With Etsy's marketing tools, you can create a comprehensive marketing strategy tailored to your unique shop and products. Whether you're just starting or looking to take your shop to the next level, Etsy's marketing tools are your ticket to success in the thriving marketplace of creative entrepreneurs.

Using Etsy's marketing tools can significantly enhance your visibility and reach on the platform. Below are some marketing t how you can enable them.

1. Promoted Listings:

Access the "Marketing" tab in your Etsy Seller Dashboard, Select "Promoted Listings" and choose the products you want to promote, Set your daily budget and maximum cost-per-click (CPC) bid for each product. Target relevant keywords that potential customers are likely to use in their searches. Monitor the performance of your promoted listings regularly and adjust bids for optimal results.

2. Etsy Ads (formerly Offsite Ads):

Enable Etsy Ads in your Marketing settings to participate in the offsite advertising program. Set your daily budget based on your advertising goals and available funds. Etsy will automatically promote your listings on external platforms like Google, Facebook, and Instagram. You pay an advertising fee only when you make a sale from an offsite ad.

3. Social Media Integration:

Connect your Etsy shop to your social media accounts like Instagram, Facebook, and Pinterest. Share your listings and shop updates directly from Etsy to your social media profiles. Use engaging visuals and compelling captions to attract potential buyers.

4.   Shop Updates:

Utilize the "Shop Updates" feature to showcase your new products, promotions, or behind-the-scenes content. Engage with your audience and encourage interaction through likes, comments, and shares.

5.   Marketing Dashboard:

Access the "Marketing" tab on your Etsy Seller Dashboard to monitor the performance of your marketing efforts, Analyze data on clicks, views, conversions, and sales attributed to your promoted listings and Etsy Ads. Use the insights to refine your marketing strategies and optimize your ad spending.

6.   Consider Seasonal and Trending Opportunities:

Align your marketing efforts with seasonal events, holidays, and popular trends to attract more customers. Create themed promotions or product collections to cater to specific buyer interests.

7.   Optimize Product Listings:

Use relevant and specific keywords in your product titles, descriptions, and tags to improve search visibility. Provide accurate and detailed product information to help customers make informed decisions.

8.   Customer Engagement:

Respond promptly to customer inquiries and reviews to provide excellent customer service. Encourage satisfied customers to leave positive reviews, which can boost your shop's credibility.

9. Continuous Evaluation and Adjustment:

Regularly review the performance of your marketing campaigns using the marketing dashboard. Adjust your strategies based on data insights, optimizing your ad budgets and targeting.

By effectively utilizing Etsy's marketing tools, you can attract more potential customers, increase sales, and grow your Etsy business successfully. Regularly monitor the performance of your marketing efforts, adapt your strategies, and stay engaged with your audience to maintain a thriving shop on Etsy.

PROMOTING YOUR SHOP ON SOCIAL MEDIA

Unlock the full potential of your Etsy shop with the magic of social media! Social media platforms like Instagram, Facebook, and Pinterest offer endless opportunities to showcase your unique products and connect with your target audience. Follow these tried-and-true strategies to effectively promote your Etsy shop on social media:

Build a Strong Brand Presence: Create a cohesive and recognizable brand identity across all your social media profiles. Use your shop's logo, colors, and style to ensure consistency and help customers identify your brand instantly.

Share Stunning Visuals: High-quality and eye-catching visuals are key to capturing your audience's attention. Use professional product images that showcase your items in the best light, and consider lifestyle or styled photos to demonstrate product usage.

Engage and Interact: Be active on social media by responding to comments, messages, and mentions promptly. Engage with your followers by asking questions, running polls, and encouraging conversations around your products.

Storytelling and Behind-the-Scenes: Share engaging stories about your creative journey, design process, and the inspiration behind your products. Showcasing the human side of your brand can build stronger connections with your audience.

Promote Exclusive Offers: Reward your social media followers with special promotions, discounts, or limited-time offers. This can create a sense of urgency and encourage them to make a purchase from your Etsy shop.

Utilize Hashtags Wisely: Research relevant and trending hashtags that resonate with your brand and products. Hashtags can expand the reach of your posts to a wider audience interested in your niche.

Cross-Promote with Influencers or Collaborators: Partner with influencers or collaborate with complementary brands to reach new audiences. Influencers can help promote your products to their followers, increasing your shop's exposure.

Pinterest for Inspiration and Traffic: Pinterest is a treasu discovering inspiration and driving traffic to your Etsy sh visually appealing pins with direct links to your product listir access.

Facebook and Instagram Ads: Utilize Facebook Ads Manager to run targeted ads on both Facebook and Instagram. Tailor your audience demographics and interests to reach potential buyers who align with your products.

Analytics and Insights: Leverage social media analytics tools to track your performance, monitor engagement, and understand your audience's preferences. Use the data to refine your strategies and content.

Remember, consistency is key. Maintain an active presence on social media, post regularly, and stay engaged with your followers. By leveraging the power of social media to promote your Etsy shop, you can unlock a world of opportunities and take your business to new heights."

RUNNING ADVERTISING CAMPAIGNS

Running advertising campaigns is an effective way to increase visibility, attract potential customers, and drive sales for your Etsy shop. Etsy offers two primary advertising tools: Promoted Listings and Etsy Ads.

Promoted Listings

Promoted Listings allow you to pay for increased visibility within Etsy's search results and related product listings. Choose the products you want to promote, set a daily budget, and bid on keywords relevant to your products.

When a shopper searches for or views products related to your chosen keywords, your promoted listings will appear at the top of the search results or in relevant product listings. You only pay when a shopper clicks on your promoted listing (cost-per-click or CPC).

Regularly monitor the performance of your promoted listings using Etsy's Ads Manager, and adjust bids and budgets to optimize results.

Etsy Ads (formerly Offsite Ads)

With Etsy Ads, your products can be promoted on external platforms like Google, Facebook, Instagram, and Pinterest, reaching an even broader audience beyond Etsy. If you're eligible, you can choose to participate in Etsy Ads, and Etsy will automatically promote your listings on these external platforms. You pay an advertising fee only when a shopper clicks on your ad and makes a purchase within 30 days (cost-per-sale or CPS). Set a daily budget for Etsy Ads to control your spending.

Determine the specific objectives of your advertising campaign. Are you aiming to increase brand awareness, drive traffic to your Etsy shop, or boost sales of specific products?

Choose the Right Advertising Platform: Select the advertising platform that aligns with your target audience and campaign goals. Popular options include Etsy Ads (formerly Promoted Listings), Facebook Ads, Instagram Ads, Google Ads, and Pinterest Ads.

Set a Budget: Determine the budget you're willing to allocate to your advertising campaign. Start with a budget that aligns with your goals and adjust it as you assess the campaign's performance.

Target Your Audience: Identify your target audience based on demographics, interests, and behavior. Use targeting options provided by the advertising platform to reach potential customers who are likely to be interested in your products.

Craft Compelling Ad Copy: Write engaging ad copy that clearly communicates the value of your products and encourages viewers to take action. Use clear calls-to-action (CTAs) to prompt clicks or conversions.

Design Eye-Catching Visuals: Use high-quality images or videos that showcase your products in the best possible light. Visuals play a significant role in capturing the attention of your audience.

Set Up Conversion Tracking: Implement conversion tracking to measure the effectiveness of your advertising campaigns. This allows you to track sales or other desired actions resulting from your ads.

A/B Test Your Ads: Run multiple versions of your ads with slight variations in copy, visuals, or targeting to identify the most effective combination. A/B testing helps you optimize your ads for better performance.

Monitor and Optimize: Regularly monitor the performance of your advertising campaigns. Track key metrics such as click-through rates

(CTR), conversion rates, and return on ad spend (ROAS). Use the insights to optimize your ads for better results.

Adjust Your Strategy: Based on the campaign's performance, adjust your advertising strategy as needed. Optimize underperforming ads, increase budgets for successful campaigns, or try new targeting options.

Test Different Platforms: Experiment with advertising on different platforms to find which ones yield the best results for your Etsy shop. Each platform has its unique audience and advertising features.

Provide a Seamless Customer Experience: Ensure that your Etsy shop, product listings, and website (if applicable) provide a seamless and positive customer experience. Deliver excellent customer service to increase the chances of repeat business.

Running advertising campaigns requires continuous monitoring and optimization. Be patient, and remember that results may take time to show. Regularly assess the performance of your campaigns, make data-driven decisions, and refine your strategy to achieve the best possible outcomes for your Etsy shop.

SECTION 4

GROWING YOUR ETSY BUSINESS.

Growing your business on Etsy can be a fulfilling endeavor for creative entrepreneurs and artisans. Here are some key points to help you succeed on this popular online marketplace:

Create a Captivating Shop: Invest time in setting up an attractive and well-organized shop. Use high-quality images and engaging product descriptions to entice potential customers.

Focus on Niche Products: Stand out from the crowd by offering unique and niche products. Specializing in a particular category can help target a specific audience and build a loyal customer base.

Optimize for Search: Etsy's search algorithm relies on keywords. Research relevant keywords and incorporate them into your titles and tags to improve the visibility of your listings.

Competitive Pricing: Price your products competitively while ensuring you maintain a healthy profit margin. Consider factors like material costs, time invested, and market demand.

Provide Excellent Customer Service: Respond promptly to customer inquiries and address any issues or concerns professionally. Positive reviews and customer satisfaction are crucial for building a strong reputation.

Promote Your Shop: Utilize social media platforms and email marketing to promote your Etsy shop and reach a broader audience. Engaging with potential customers can lead to increased traffic and sales.

Offer Special Deals: Occasional sales, discounts, or limited-time offers can attract more customers and encourage repeat business.

Use Etsy Advertising: Experiment with Etsy Ads to boost the visibility of your listings. Monitor their performance and adjust your strategy accordingly.

Stay Updated with Trends: Keep an eye on market trends and adapt your product offerings and marketing strategies accordingly.

Participate in the Etsy Community: Join Etsy teams and forums to connect with other sellers, share insights, and gain support. Collaborating with others can open up new opportunities.

Track Shop Analytics: Utilize Etsy's analytics tools to gain valuable insights into your shop's performance, customer behavior, and popular products. Use this data to make informed business decisions.

Maintain High-Quality Standards: Consistently deliver high-quality products and maintain professional customer service. Positive reviews and customer satisfaction are vital for long-term success.

Remember, growing a business on Etsy takes time and effort. Stay persistent, adapt to changes, and continuously improve your shop and products. By combining creativity, passion, and strategic efforts, you can create a thriving business on Etsy.

EXPANDING YOUR PRODUCT LINE

Expanding your product line on Etsy is a great way to attract more customers, increase sales, and diversify your offerings. In this Guide are steps to effectively expand your product line on Etsy.

Market Research: Begin by conducting market research to identify potential gaps and opportunities in your niche. Look for products that complement your existing offerings and align with your target audience's preferences.

Understand Customer Needs: Listen to your customers' feedback and reviews to understand their needs and preferences better. This information can guide you in developing products that cater to their desires.

Product Development: Once you've identified product ideas, focus on developing them with quality materials and craftsmanship. Keep your branding consistent to maintain a cohesive image for your shop.

Start Small: Introduce new products gradually, rather than overwhelming your shop with a large number of items all at once. Starting small allows you to gauge the demand for new products and make adjustments accordingly.

Photography and Descriptions: Ensure that your new product listings have high-quality images and compelling descriptions. Good photography and clear product details are crucial for attracting potential buyers.

Pricing Strategy: Set competitive prices for your new products while considering factors like production costs, market demand, and competitor pricing. Avoid underpricing your items as it may devalue your brand.

Promote New Products: Utilize your existing customer base and social media presence to promote your new products. Engage with your audience and create excitement around the new additions to your shop.

Offer Bundles and Sets: Consider creating bundles or sets that include both existing and new products. Bundling can encourage customers to purchase multiple items at once, increasing your average order value.

Stay True to Your Brand: Ensure that the new products align with your brand's identity and aesthetic. A consistent brand image helps build trust and recognition among customers.

Monitor Performance: Keep a close eye on how your new products perform. Use Etsy's analytics to track sales, views, and customer behavior. This data will guide you in refining your product line over time.

Customer Feedback: Encourage customers to leave reviews and feedback for your new products. This input is valuable for understanding how well the products are received and making improvements if needed.

Stay Innovative: Continue to innovate and evolve your product line to stay relevant and meet changing customer preferences. Regularly introduce new items to keep your shop fresh and engaging.

By expanding your product line thoughtfully and strategically, you can attract a broader customer base and create more opportunities for growth and success on Etsy. Remember to balance innovation with customer demand, and always prioritize quality and customer satisfaction in all your endeavors.

OFFERING DISCOUNTS AND PROMOTIONS

Offering discounts and promotions is a powerful marketing strategy to attract customers, increase sales, and create a sense of urgency. Offer a percentage off the regular price, such as 10% or 20% off. This type of discount is easy to understand and appeals to customers seeking a deal.

Provide a specific dollar amount off the total purchase, like $5 or $10 off. This can be particularly effective for encouraging higher-value purchases. Offer free shipping on select products or for orders that meet a certain minimum purchase amount. Many customers find free shipping attractive and are more likely to complete their purchase.

Implement a "Buy One, Get One" promotion, where customers receive a free or discounted item when they purchase another. Create a sense of urgency by running time-limited sales, such as a "Flash Sale" or "Weekend Sale." Limited-time offers encourage customers to act quickly to take advantage of the discount.

Align your promotions with holidays, seasons, or special occasions. For example, offer discounts for Valentine's Day, Black Friday, or Christmas. Attract new customers by offering exclusive discounts or promo codes for their first purchase.

Encourage word-of-mouth marketing by implementing a referral program. Offer discounts or rewards to customers who refer new customers to your shop. Reward loyal customers with discounts or special offers after they reach a certain spending threshold or make a specific number of purchases.

Send personalized discount codes to customers who abandoned their shopping carts to incentivize them to complete their purchase. Run exclusive promotions or offer discount codes to your social media followers to engage your audience and drive traffic to your shop.

Encourage customers to sign up for your email newsletter by offering a discount on their next purchase. This helps you build a loyal customer base and keep them informed about future promotions.

When offering discounts and promotions, it's essential to set clear terms and conditions, including the expiration date, eligible products, and any other limitations. Monitor the performance of your promotions using analytics to evaluate their effectiveness and adjust your strategies as needed. By using discounts and promotions strategically, you can drive sales, retain customers, and create a positive shopping experience for your audience.

COLLABORATING WITH OTHER SELLERS.

Collaborating with other sellers on Etsy can be a mutually beneficial strategy that opens up new opportunities, fosters growth, and enhances your shop's visibility and credibility. Collaborating with sellers who offer complementary products can lead to the creation of product bundles or sets. Bundling products together can increase the perceived value for customers and encourage them to purchase multiple items at once. This not only boosts your average order value but also introduces your products to the collaborating seller's customer base.

Partnering with other sellers to cross-promote each other's products can expand your reach to a broader audience. You can feature each other's products in your shop announcements, social media posts, newsletters, or through promotional events. This cross-promotion can lead to increased exposure and potentially bring in new customers. Create themed collections by curating products from different sellers that share a common theme, style, or occasion. Collaborative collections can be featured on each seller's shop, and it allows you to showcase a wider range of products to customers interested in that specific theme.

Pooling resources with other sellers to invest in marketing initiatives can be more cost-effective and impactful. You can jointly fund online advertising, sponsor events, or collaborate on influencer marketing campaigns, reaching a larger audience collectively. Building relationships with other sellers can create a supportive community where you can share insights, experiences, and advice. Learning from each other's successes and challenges can help you improve your business strategies and navigate the dynamic Etsy marketplace better.

Etsy offers "Teams," which are groups of sellers with shared interests or niches. Joining a Team allows you to connect with like-minded sellers and participate in team-specific events, promotions, and collaborative efforts. Being part of a Team can increase your shop's exposure within the Etsy community. Collaborating with other sellers to purchase supplies in bulk can result in cost savings and discounts. Bulk purchasing allows you to secure better deals on materials and reduce production costs, which can positively impact your pricing and profit margins.

If you and another seller are shipping products to the same location or event, collaborating on shipping costs can help both of you save money. It's especially useful for sellers attending craft fairs or events where they can share booth space and logistics. Establishing a referral system with other sellers can lead to mutual customer referrals. When a customer purchases from one shop, they may receive information about other related sellers and vice versa. This increases the chances of attracting repeat business and expanding your customer base.

Remember that successful collaborations are built on trust, communication, and a shared vision. Be selective about who you collaborate with and ensure that your values and products align well. By collaborating with other sellers, you can tap into new markets, strengthen your brand, and foster a sense of community that benefits everyone involved.

ATTENDING CRAFTS FAIRS AND OTHER EVENTS.

Craft fairs are events where artisans, makers, and sellers gather to showcase and sell their handmade or unique products directly to customers. These fairs provide an excellent opportunity for small businesses and independent artists to interact with their target audience, build brand visibility, and make sales on the spot. If you're considering participating in craft fairs, there are specific things you should look forward to.

RESEARCH AND PLANNING

Conduct thorough research to identify craft fairs that align with your target market and product niche. Look for events that attract your ideal customers and have a good track record of attendance and sales. Once you've identified potential fairs, review their application process and deadlines. Some craft fairs require early applications due to high demand. Consider the cost of booth fees, travel, accommodation, and the necessary display materials. Create a budget to ensure you can participate without stretching your resources too thin.

PREPARING YOUR BOOTH

Plan a layout that maximizes the use of your space and allows customers to navigate your booth easily. Use tables, shelves, and displays to showcase your products effectively. Design eye-catching signage and banners that reflect your brand and attract attention from a distance. Adequate lighting can make your products stand out and create an inviting atmosphere within your booth. Invest in professional and sturdy display materials that enhance the presentation of your products.

INVENTORY PACKAGING

Ensure you have enough stock to meet demand throughout the duration of the fair. Bring a variety of products to cater to different customer preferences. Have attractive and professional packaging for your products, making them ready for gifting if needed.

MARKETING AND PROMOTION

Leverage your social media channels, website, and email newsletter to inform your existing audience about your participation in the craft fair. Create excitement and anticipation for the event. Prepare business cards, brochures, or postcards with your booth number and contact information to distribute to potential customers.

PRICING AND PAYMENT

Clearly label the prices of your products. Consider offering various price points to accommodate different budgets. Accept multiple payment options, such as cash, credit/debit cards, and mobile payments, to provide a seamless shopping experience for customers.

ENGAGING CUSTOMERS

Greet visitors with a friendly and welcoming attitude. Engage them in conversations and show genuine interest in their needs and preferences. Share the stories and inspirations behind your products. Customers appreciate the personal touch and connection to the maker.

TRACKING AND FOLLOW UP

Keep a record of your sales and customer interactions during the fair. This information will be valuable for future analysis and decision-making. After the event, follow up with potential leads and customers by sending thank-you emails or special offers to continue building relationships. Evaluate your sales and calculate the return on investment (ROI) to determine if the craft fair was profitable for your business.

Consider customer feedback and observations to identify areas for improvement in your booth setup, product offerings, and customer experience.

Participating in craft fairs can be a rewarding experience for artisans and sellers. By conducting thorough research, preparing well, and engaging with customers effectively, you can make the most of these events to grow your brand, expand your customer base, and generate sales for your business. Regularly refine your approach based on insights from each fair, and continue participating in events that align with your business goals and target market.

FAQS

As an Etsy seller, you may encounter a variety of questions from potential buyers or other sellers. Here are some frequently asked questions on Etsy:

1.   How do I purchase an item on Etsy?

Answer: To purchase an item on Etsy, simply click on the listing you're interested in, select any variations (if applicable), and click the "Add to Cart" button. When you're ready to complete your purchase, click on the shopping cart icon at the top right of the page and follow the checkout process.

2.   Do you offer international shipping?

Answer: This question is commonly asked by buyers outside of the seller's country. As a seller, you can choose to offer international shipping or limit your shipping to specific regions.

3.   Can I customize this item?

Answer: Many buyers are interested in personalized or customized items. Sellers can respond by providing options for customization, either in the listing or through direct messages.

4. What are your shipping times?

Answer: Buyers want to know when they can expect their order to arrive. As a seller, it's essential to provide accurate shipping times and set realistic expectations for delivery.

5. What is your return policy?

Answer: Buyers may ask about your shop's return and refund policies. Clearly outline your policies in your shop's "Policies" section to avoid any confusion.

6. Do I track my order?

Answer: Provide buyers with information on how they can track their order once it has been shipped. Etsy's integrated tracking system can help with this.

7. Are your products handmade?

Answer: If you sell handmade items, buyers may inquire about the process and materials used. Be prepared to share information about your craft and creative process.

8. Can I get a discount for bulk orders?

Answer: Some buyers may be interested in ordering multiple quantities of your products at once. Be ready to discuss bulk order discounts or any other special offers you provide.

9. What payment methods do you accept?

Answer: Make sure to list the payment methods you accept, whether it's through Etsy's integrated payment system or other options like PayPal.

10. Can I cancel my order?

Answer: Buyers may want to know about your order cancellation policy. Be clear about under what circumstances orders can be canceled and how to request cancellations.

11. Do you offer gift wrapping?

Answer: Some buyers may want to have their purchases gift-wrapped. If you provide gift wrapping services, mention it in your shop's listings or policies.

12. How can I contact you for further questions?

Answer: Always provide contact information, such as an email address or Etsy's messaging system, so buyers can easily reach out to you with any additional queries they may have.

Being prepared to answer these common questions in a friendly and informative manner can help you provide excellent customer service and encourage potential buyers to make a purchase from your Etsy shop.

GLOSSARY

KEY TERMS FOR BUYERS AND SELLERS

This glossary includes key terms relevant to both buyers and sellers on Etsy. Understanding these terms will help users navigate the platform and enhance their overall experience when buying and selling unique handmade and vintage products.

Etsy: An online marketplace that specializes in handmade, vintage, and craft supplies. It allows individuals and businesses to buy and sell unique and creative products.

Listing: A product or item that a seller has listed for sale on Etsy. Each listing typically includes product details, photos, pricing, and shipping information.

Handmade: Items that are created, designed, or crafted by the seller personally, without the use of mass production techniques.

Vintage: Products that are at least 20 years old and are considered collectible or of nostalgic value.

Customization: The option for buyers to request personalized modifications or alterations to an item before purchasing.

Shop Policies: The seller's guidelines and rules regarding shipping, returns, refunds, and other important information for buyers.

Favourites(Faves): The heart-shaped button on Etsy that buyers use to save and bookmark items or shops they are interested in.

Cart: The virtual shopping cart where buyers can add items they want to purchase before proceeding to checkout.

Checkout: The process where buyers provide shipping information, select a payment method, and complete the purchase of the items in their cart.

Convo: Short for "conversation," it refers to Etsy's messaging system, where buyers and sellers can communicate with each other.

Feedbacks: Reviews and ratings left by buyers after completing a purchase, reflecting their overall experience with the seller and the product.

Tags: Keywords or phrases that sellers use to describe their products, making them easier for buyers to find in Etsy's search results.

SEO: Search Engine Optimization, the process of optimizing listings and shop content to improve their visibility in search results.

Promoted Listing: A paid advertising feature that allows sellers to promote their products to a larger audience within Etsy's search and browse results.

Bulk Order: A large quantity of items purchased by a buyer, often at a discounted rate.

Reserved Listing: An item that a seller sets aside for a specific buyer who has requested it.

Featured Seller: A shop or seller chosen by Etsy for special recognition and promotion on the platform.

On Vacation Mode: When a seller temporarily closes their shop for a specific period, typically to catch up on orders or take a break.

Digital Download: Products that can be purchased and downloaded directly from the shop, such as printables, digital art, or templates.

Abandoned Cart: When a buyer adds items to their cart but does not complete the purchase, leaving the items "abandoned" in the cart.

Printed in Great Britain
by Amazon

32085125R00051